Waste and Recycling

A & C Black · London

Contents

Just throw it away   4
Sorting out rubbish, packaging materials, how much rubbish
we throw away

Rotten rubbish   7
Why natural materials rot away in the soil, leaf litter,
compost heaps

Litter on the streets   10
Why litter is dangerous, litter bins, clearing up litter

Collecting rubbish   11
Refuse collection vehicles and street cleaners

Dumping rubbish   12
Burying rubbish under the ground, gas given off by rotting
rubbish, soil pollution

Burning rubbish   13
Burning rubbish at high temperatures in incinerators, using
the heat to make electricity

Poisonous waste   14
Chemical waste, nuclear waste and oil, birds with oil on
their feathers

Cover photographs
Front – Looking at life in leaf litter (see p. 8).
Back – Selling sandals made from car tyres in Bolivia
(see p. 31).
Title page – Using a magnet to separate metals from
other rubbish (see p. 26).

Acknowledgements
Edited by Barbara Taylor
Photographs by Jenny Matthews except for:
p.5 (left) Morgan, p.17 (top) Meech, (bottom)
Wilkinson, p.29 (inset) Morgan, Ecoscene;
p.12, p.14 Cleanaway; p.28 Ed Barber.

The author and publisher would like to thank the
following people for their invaluable help and
advice during the preparation of this book:
The staff and pupils at Dog Kennel Hill School;
Cleanaway; The Tidy Britain Group.

A CIP catalogue record for this book is available
from the British Library.

ISBN 0–7136–3809–5

First paperback edition 1993

First published 1990 in hardback by
A & C Black (Publishers) Ltd
35 Bedford Row, London WC1R 4JH

© 1993, 1990 A & C Black (Publishers) Limited

Animal rubbish 16
Dung and droppings, dog dirt

Watery waste 17
Where sewage comes from, cleaning up sewage so the water can be recycled

Recycling rubbish 18
Using things again or making new things from rubbish

Getting rid of rubbish 19
Summary of all the ways we get rid of rubbish

The second half of this book is about recycling different materials.

Paper 20
Cans 24
Scrap metals 26
Glass 27
Plastics 29
Old clothes 30
New things from old 31
Useful addresses 32
Index 32

Typeset by August Filmsetting, Haydock, St Helens
Printed in Italy by Amadeus

Remember to wash your hands after doing any experiments with rubbish or rotten materials.

Earthwatch books in hardback

Clean Air Dirty Air	People or Wildlife?
Food for Thought	The Urban Environment
Trees for Tomorrow	Fuelling the Future
Waste and Recycling	Water for Life

Just throw it away

Packets, cans, jars, bottles, cartons – what sort of rubbish do you throw away every day? The amount of rubbish each one of us throws away in a month weighs nearly as much as a person. Think how much all the rubbish from your home or school would weigh in a year.

Yet this rubbish is only a tiny part of all the rubbish produced by people. There is the rubbish and dirty water from shops, offices, hotels and hospitals as well as the litter dropped on the streets. There is the waste produced by factories when they make different products. Some of this waste may be poisonous. There is the broken rock and dirty soil produced by quarries and mines. And there is the waste produced when farmers grow crops or keep farm animals.

On this rubbish tip in Guatemala, the people are searching for waste materials that can be used again or made into new things. This is called recycling. Up to 75% of all the waste we produce could be recycled.

Do we need to make so much rubbish?

If you unwrapped everything from a weekly visit to the supermarket all at once, you would end up with a very large pile of rubbish. All these wrappings, boxes and trays are called packaging. Packaging keeps food fresh, stops things getting squashed or broken and gives information about what's inside. But is it all necessary?

When you go shopping, it's a good idea to take your own bags with you instead of getting new ones each time. How many times can you re-use a bag before it breaks? Can you think of a way of testing bags to see how strong they are? This picture might give you some ideas.

Sorting out rubbish

Ask an adult for a bag full of household rubbish. Put on some plastic or rubber gloves and sort out the rubbish into sets of materials, such as paper, food scraps, plastics, metals and glass.

Weigh each set of material and record the weights on a chart. Which material weighs the most? Compare your results with the chart below.

Weighing rubbish is only one way of measuring waste. It can give you misleading results. For instance, plastics are not very heavy, but they take up a lot of space. Try measuring how much space each kind of material takes up. How are your results different?

Weight of rubbish in a modern household rubbish bin

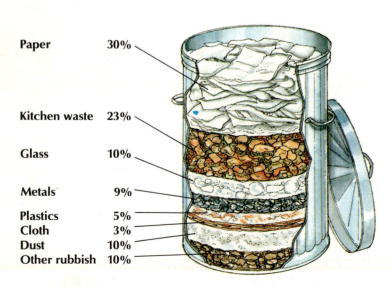

Paper	30%
Kitchen waste	23%
Glass	10%
Metals	9%
Plastics	5%
Cloth	3%
Dust	10%
Other rubbish	10%

Fifty years ago, people threw away a lot of food scraps, vegetable peelings and huge amounts of ash and cinders from coal and wood fires. Nowadays, there is much less ash because of central heating. There is also less waste from fresh vegetables because people eat more frozen and prepared foods. But there is a lot more food packaging.

Rotten rubbish

A lot of the rubbish we throw away is buried in the soil.
What happens to the different materials when they are under
the ground? Try this test to find out.

Burying rubbish

1 Collect some different man-made materials, such as a glass marble, a rubber balloon, polystyrene and tin foil. Find some natural materials such as fruit and paper.

2 Fill some pots with soil and bury one kind of material in each pot. Label each pot with the name of the material and the date.

3 Pour some water on to the soil in each pot.

4 After a week or more, dig up each material. Has it changed?

The soil is full of small animals, microscopic bacteria, and tiny plants called fungi, which feed on natural materials and break them down. The materials eventually become part of the bodies of living things or part of the soil.

Living things that feed on dead or decaying materials are called decomposers. The materials they eat are said to be biodegradable, which means 'able to be broken down by living things'. Unfortunately, decomposers do not eat man-made materials. So these materials stay in the soil and do not change.

Catch some decomposers

1 Collect leaf litter from under trees or hedges.

2 Put some damp blotting paper in a large jar and wrap a piece of black paper around the outside of the jar.

3 Fit a funnel in the top of the jar and fill the funnel with leaf litter.

4 Shine a light on to the leaf litter and leave it for a few hours. The light dries out the litter and tiny animals in the litter try to get away from the dryness and the heat of the light. Some of them will fall into the jar.

5 Take off the black paper and look at the animals in the jar with a magnifying glass. Draw the animals you see and try to find out their names.

6 When you have finished, put the leaf litter back where you found it and wash your hands.

How many different decomposers did you discover? Look out for soil creatures such as worms, beetles, woodlice and springtails. Did you find white threads on any of the leaves? These are the feeding threads of fungi. Bacteria are too small to see with your magnifying glass. But there are millions of them in a funnel of leaf litter. Bacteria and fungi are the most important decomposers of dead leaves and other biodegradable rubbish.

Build a compost heap

If you have a garden or an allotment, you can use plant and animal decomposers to turn the waste from plants into stuff called compost. This is natural rubbish that has rotted down. It can be mixed in with soil to make it rich and help plants to grow. If you get rid of your plant rubbish like this, it will also help to stop your rubbish bin from smelling.

1 Collect waste plant materials

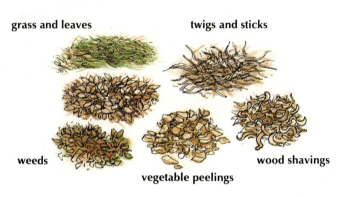

grass and leaves

twigs and sticks

weeds

vegetable peelings

wood shavings

2 Ask an adult to help you build a compost bin – or buy one. Put the bin in a shady place out of the way.

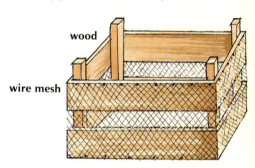

wood

wire mesh

3 Put the different wastes into the bin in layers. Make each layer about 15–20 cm deep.

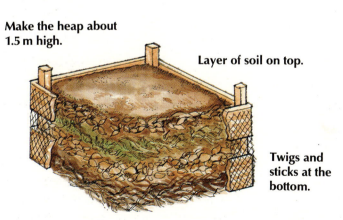

Make the heap about 1.5 m high.

Layer of soil on top.

Twigs and sticks at the bottom.

4 Water the heap and cover it with a piece of old carpet or a lid to keep in the heat.

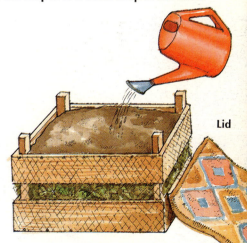

Lid

Leave the compost heap for a few months, making sure it does not dry out. As decomposers eat the rubbish, the compost will heat up. It can be up to 66°C in the middle of a large heap. You may even see steam rising from the heap. When the rubbish has rotted down, you can dig it into the soil in the vegetable patch or flower beds.

Litter on the streets

Litter can be as small as a sweet wrapping or as big as an old mattress. Apart from looking nasty and making places unpleasant to live in, litter can also be very dangerous. Litter carries germs and diseases. It can pollute the soil and injure people and animals. Many animals die from eating plastic bags.

How much litter is there in your area? Carry out a litter survey with your friends. Draw a map and mark the places that have the most litter. Dropping litter is against the law but the law is hard to enforce and people are rarely fined.

▲ Are there enough litter bins in your area? What is the best shape for a litter bin?

▼ This piece of waste ground has been cleared of litter and now provides a home for all kinds of wildlife.

Collecting rubbish

▲ Rubbish collection can be dirty and dangerous work. Never go near a refuse collection vehicle.

Who collects all the litter and rubbish we throw away? Street cleaners or small rubbish collection vehicles clean up litter on the streets. The rubbish from people's homes is usually collected about once a week by a team of people with a refuse collection vehicle. Many of these vehicles have a special machine inside to press the rubbish down tightly so it takes up less space.

Rubbish from blocks of flats, schools, offices, shops, hospitals and factories is put into large bins or skips. The whole bin or skip is lifted up and taken away to be emptied. This way, a lot of rubbish can be collected at once.

▶ Street cleaners sweep the pavements and gutters and empty the litter bins.

▲ This rubbish collection vehicle runs on electricity. Unlike a vehicle with a petrol engine, it does not produce harmful fumes which pollute the air.

Dumping rubbish

What happens to all the rubbish we collect? Where does it go? A lot of it is used to fill in holes in the ground, such as quarries. These are called 'landfill' sites. Every day, a layer of soil is put on top of the rubbish. This helps to stop birds and animals, such as rats, from feeding and breeding on the mounds of rubbish. The birds and animals can spread germs and diseases.

After some years, the land above the site can be used for some kinds of buildings, recreation, woodland or farming. Landfill sites are the cheapest way to get rid of rubbish. But the sites are often a long way from towns and cities and transport is expensive. It also damages the environment. Landfill sites can also cause pollution if poisonous wastes, such as the mercury from batteries, 'leak out' of the site into the soil.

▲ The rubbish on a landfill site is spread out by a bulldozer and squashed by heavy vehicles so it takes up less space and is less likely to blow away. This helps to stop the rubbish heating up like a compost heap and cuts down the risk of fires.

▼ Inside a landfill site, a gas called methane is often produced as the rubbish rots away. On this site, the methane is being burnt so it will not cause an explosion. Methane does not have to be wasted. It can be used for heating.

Burning rubbish

Another way to get rid of rubbish is to burn it in a large machine called an incinerator. Only a small amount of rubbish is burnt in this way because it is expensive to build and run incinerators. The heat from the burning rubbish can be used to heat homes or produce electrical power.

After rubbish has been burnt, only a small amount of waste is left. This will not spread disease. It can be recycled and used again – to build roads, for example. But if an incinerator is not working properly or does not burn the rubbish at a high enough temperature, smoke and harmful gases from the chimney can pollute the air.

▼ At this incinerator, the refuse collection vehicles tip their rubbish into huge bunkers. A crane then grabs the rubbish and lifts it into chutes leading to the boilers.

▲ In the control room, scientists check that the boilers are working properly. Inside the boilers, the rubbish is burnt at very high temperatures – from 925–1040°C. The heat from the burning rubbish turns water into steam, which is used to make electricity.

Poisonous waste

Poisonous waste, such as chemicals, oil and nuclear waste, needs special treatment. Chemical waste can be destroyed in incinerators at very high temperatures. It can also be buried underground in strong, sealed containers. But it is hard to be sure the poisons will not seep out to pollute the environment in the future.

The waste from nuclear power stations is a very difficult problem because it is so dangerous and the radioactivity it gives off lasts for such a long time. Some will give off radiation for hundreds of thousands of years.

Nuclear waste has to be stored or buried somewhere until it stops giving off radiation. But scientists still need to find out more about how the nuclear waste might affect the environment after it is buried.

▲ High temperature incinerators are used to get rid of dangerous wastes, such as those produced by the chemical and electrical industries. Before waste is burnt in an incinerator, scientists test the waste to find out more about the properties of the chemicals it contains.

▼ This scientist is checking the soil to see if an incinerator is affecting the local environment.

Oil

Have you ever seen lumps of black tar on a beach? They may have come from a ship that has dumped waste oil into the sea, or from an oil tanker that has been in an accident. Apart from making the beach dirty, the oil is very dangerous to animals, especially birds.

Oil and feathers

Lay two feathers on some blotting paper and put a few drops of bicycle oil on each feather. Dip cotton wool into some washing-up liquid and clean up one of the feathers.

Put drops of water onto the two feathers and on to a clean feather. What shape are the water drops on each feather? Which feather is best at keeping out the water?

Feather with oil

Clean feather

Feather with oil washed off

On a clean feather, the water forms round drops and rolls off the surface. On an oily feather, the water soaks in. Oily feathers stick together and do not keep out the cold and wet. A seabird with oily feathers cannot dive underwater and catch fish. The birds die from cold and hunger. They may also be poisoned if they swallow oil.

If there is not too much oil on their feathers, birds can be washed with warm water and detergent and released in a place where there is no oil pollution. Did you manage to clean up the oily feather and make it waterproof again?

Animal rubbish

A lot of natural waste is produced by animals. In a natural system, all the dung and droppings from animals are eaten up by decomposers and the goodness goes back into the soil. But people keep a lot of animals together on farms, and these large amounts of waste can be hard to get rid of.

In some countries, animal, human and plant wastes are put into very large containers called bio-gas chambers. These chambers are sealed so the air cannot get in. Inside a bio-gas chamber, the wastes break down and give off methane gas. The gas can be used for heating, lighting, cooking or driving machines. Any waste that is leftover at the end of the process can be used to help the crops to grow. Bio-gas chambers cut down the risk of disease because dangerous bacteria are killed off inside the chamber.

Bio-gas chamber

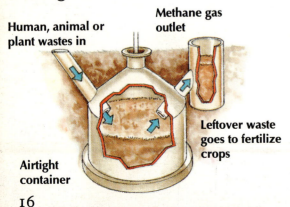

Methane gas outlet

Human, animal or plant wastes in

Leftover waste goes to fertilize crops

Airtight container

▲ Animal dung can be dried in the sun and then burnt to provide heat for cooking.

▼ Dog dirt makes streets and parks unpleasant to walk in. It can also spread diseases. This sign tells people that dogs are not allowed. Do you think dogs should be kept in towns?

Watery waste

Every time you pull out the plug in the bath or flush the toilet, you are producing more waste. All the watery waste from homes, offices, factories and streets is called sewage. It contains millions of bacteria and tiny creatures that cause infections and diseases.

At a sewage works, the water is cleaned before it is put back into rivers, lakes or the sea. This recycles the water so it can be used again.

Some of the solid wastes produced during the cleaning process can be spread on the fields to help the crops to grow.

▼ In some countries, sewage from towns on the coast is pumped into the sea. Longer pipes carry the sewage further out to sea and help to stop the beaches becoming polluted with sewage. Over time, seawater is supposed to kill germs and make sewage harmless. But scientists still need to find out more about the effect of sewage on the plants and animals that live in the sea.

Recycling rubbish

Getting rid of all the waste we produce is a big problem. A lot of the materials we throw away can be recycled and used again. If we recycled more of our rubbish, it would help to solve the problem of waste disposal and cause less damage to the environment.

Using the special containers at recycling centres, rubbish is separated into different types ready for recycling.

Recycling old materials means that less new materials are needed. For instance, recycling paper means that less trees have to be cut down. Making things from recycled materials uses less energy and causes less pollution than using the original raw materials (see page 20).

▲ In some countries, people go round the streets with small carts collecting metals and other materials that can be recycled.

Getting rid of rubbish

Can you remember all the different ways we get rid of our rubbish?

We bury rubbish in landfill sites.

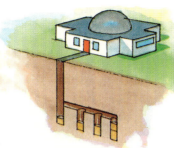

We bury poisonous waste in sealed containers under the ground.

We burn rubbish in incinerators.

We clean up sewage and put it back into rivers, lakes or the sea.

We use animal waste to help crops to grow.

We burn animal dung for heating and cooking.

We recycle some materials to make new things.

Nature can cope with natural rubbish produced by plants and animals. The materials are broken down by decomposers and used again, so nothing is wasted. But the natural system is upset by the huge amounts of rubbish produced by people. Much of our rubbish cannot be broken down by decomposers. Some of it is poisonous. It would be a good idea if we produced less waste in the first place and recylced more of the things we make.

In the rest of this book, you can find out how materials can be recycled.

Paper

Every year, each one of us uses up two trees' worth of paper and cardboard. Making paper also uses up huge amounts of energy, water and chemicals.

Making paper

1 Trees are the 'raw materials' used to make paper. We cut down trees and do not always plant enough new trees to take their place. Trees take a long time to grow.

2 To cut down trees and transport them to the factory, we use machines that run on the energy in petrol or diesel fuel.

3 Chopping up tree trunks into wood chips uses more machines and more energy.

4 To turn the wood chips into pulp, a lot of water and chemicals are needed. About half of each tree may be thrown away and wasted.

5 Poisonous wastes are produced, which may be destroyed using machines or dumped in rivers and lakes, causing pollution.

6 Wood or pulp may be imported from other countries. More energy is used up on lorries, ships and planes.

7 Lorries take the paper to places where it is needed. They use up more energy.

Making paper from recycled materials uses only half the energy and less than one third of the water needed to make paper from trees. And less harmful chemicals are released into the rivers from the paper factories. If paper is recycled, it also means there is less waste to fill up landfill sites.

Have you ever collected paper for recycling? There need to be more places for people to take waste paper. It is not worth people driving long distances to a recycling centre. The poisonous fumes from their cars will pollute the air and cause more damage to the environment than they would save by recycling paper.

What you can do

* Don't waste paper. Use both sides of each sheet wherever you can.

* Stick new labels on old envelopes and use them again.

* Use recycled paper.

* If there is a collection point near you, take your waste paper there. Fax paper, waxed or gummed paper, telephone directories and glossy magazines coated with wax or plastic or bound with strong glue cannot be recycled.

Making recycled paper

1 Tear up newspaper or tissue into small pieces. Put the paper in a bowl, add hot water and leave the paper to soak until it is really soft and mushy. Beat the mushy mixture with a whisk or ask an adult to beat the mixture in a liquidizer. This breaks up the fibres in the paper and spreads them through the water.

2 While the paper is soaking, make a sieve to drain the water from the mushy mixture. Nail four pieces of wood together to make a frame.

3 Cover the frame with fine curtain netting, wire gauze or the backing used for tapestry weaving. Fix the net or gauze in place with drawing pins or nails. Put some blotting paper on top of several layers of newspaper.

4 Lower your sieve carefully into the mushy mixture and lift it up so that the sieve is flat. Wait for most of the water to drain through.

5 Turn the sieve quickly upside down and tip the mushy paper on to the blotting paper. If any of the paper gets stuck on the sieve, press a sponge on to the back of the sieve to make the paper fall off.

6 Put another piece of blotting paper on top of the mushy paper and use a rolling pin to squeeze out some more of the water.

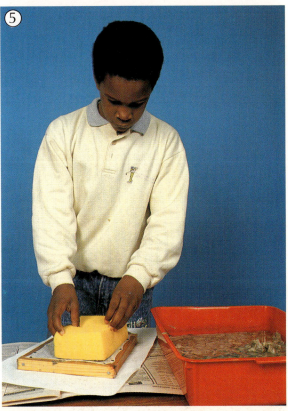

Turn the blotting paper over and ask an adult to help you iron the blotting paper until the recycled paper underneath it is nearly dry. Peel off the top piece of blotting paper and leave your recycled paper in a warm place to finish drying.

Cans

Every year, we throw away billions and billions of cans. If all the drinks cans thrown away in Britain in 1986 had been placed end to end, they would have reached the Moon. Cans are made from aluminium, steel, or steel coated with tin. Aluminium cans are light in weight but they are very strong.

Aluminium and steel come from rocks, which have to be dug up from mines. The rocks are heated at high temperatures in furnaces to make them melt. The metals can then be separated from the rocks. Making aluminium uses up six times more energy than making steel. This is partly because the process needs much higher temperatures but also because the rocks have to be 'cooked' with chemicals and treated with electricity before they are heated in the furnace.

Before cans can be recycled, the steel and aluminium cans have to be separated. This is quite easy because steel is magnetic and will stick to a magnet. Aluminium is not magnetic.

If more cans are recycled, energy will be saved and less waste will be produced. Recycling will also mean that less mines need to be dug. Mines damage the countryside and produce chemical waste, which pollutes soils and rivers.

How aluminium is recycled

1 Cans are collected, washed and squashed.

2 Cans are taken to the recycling centre.

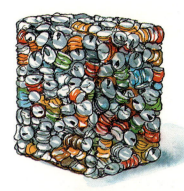

3 Cans are pressed into bales so they are easier to transport to the factory.

4 In the factory, the metal is heated until it melts and then rolled into long sheets.

5 Sheets of metal are cut up to make cans.

6 Cans are bought in a shop.

Making cans from recycled aluminium uses only 5% of the energy needed to make cans from raw aluminium.

What you can do

* Don't buy things in cans unless you have to. Buy things in bottles that can be recycled.

* Take re-usable bottles or Thermos flasks on picnics and hikes.

* If there is a collection point near you, take cans to be recycled. Wash the cans out and stamp on them to squash the sides together. This saves space and stops the cans smelling.

Scrap metals

At a scrap-yard, a large magnet on the end of a crane is used to separate out the metals from the other rubbish.

Unlike cans, quite a lot of the scrap metal from factories, buildings and homes is recycled instead of being thrown away. The metal is collected by scrap metal dealers who sort and grade the metal before breaking it up into small pieces and pressing it into bales. The bales are sent to the factory to be made into new metals. This saves energy and vital raw materials. For example, making steel from scrap uses only 25% of the energy needed to change raw materials into steel.

Car breakers collect old or damaged cars and prepare them for recycling. First they strip out any parts that can be used again, such as radiators, batteries or gearboxes. Then the empty shell is flattened with a crusher and cut into pieces.

Glass

In most homes, people throw away about five glass jars or bottles every week. Fortunately, glass can be recycled again and again. You can take your old glass to special bins called bottle banks.

Lorries empty the bottle banks and take the broken glass to a glass factory. There it is cleaned and crushed into small pieces called cullet. The cullet is used to make new bottles and jars.

What you can do

* Buy glass containers instead of plastic ones, as they are much easier to recycle.

* If there is a bottle bank near you, take your used bottles there and persuade your friends and relatives to do the same.

* Follow the bottle bank code:

– Put the bottles or jars in the correct bank for each colour.
– Put only glass bottles and jars in the banks. Other materials can damage the machines in the factory and contaminate the glass.
– Don't put bottles that can be returned into the bottle banks.
– Don't leave empty boxes or plastic bags around the bottle banks.
– Don't use the bottle banks at night. The noise may disturb people who live nearby.

How glass is recycled

1 Glass collected from bottle banks by lorries.

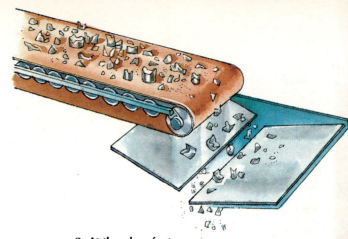

2 At the glass factory, the glass is crushed into small pieces.

3 Waste glass is mixed with soda ash, sand and limestone in a furnace and heated to 1500°C.

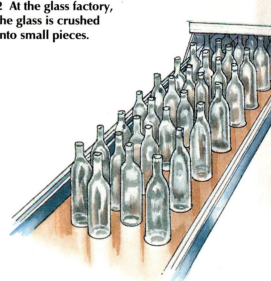

4 The runny glass goes into a mould and is blown into the shape of a new bottle or jar.

Recycling glass saves digging up the countryside to get the raw materials needed to make glass, which are sand, soda ash and limestone. And it also saves energy. Recycling a tonne of waste glass saves up to 136 litres of oil. This is partly because recycled glass melts at lower temperatures than the raw materials. But it is also because recycling saves the energy needed to produce the raw materials and deliver them to the factory.

▲ These small pieces of glass, called cullet, are ready to be made into new glass.

Plastics

This baling machine squashes plastic bottles ready for recycling.

There are over fifty different types of plastic, which are made from valuable raw materials, such as oil, gas, coal and salt. A lot of plastics are used for packaging. Most plastics do not rot and are not recycled. If they are not burnt properly in incinerators, harmful gases may be released into the air.

One of the most common plastics used in drinks bottles is called PET for short. PET can be recycled if it is kept separate from other rubbish. But it needs to be stamped with a code so it can be identified. In the United States of America, PET is recycled and used to make new products such as flower pots and milk crates.

What you can do

✳ Try and re-use your old plastic containers, for example as flower pots, for mixing paint or for storing things.

✳ Find out which plastic bottles can be refilled when they are empty and use these products.

✳ Buy products that have as little plastic packaging as possible and persuade your friends and relatives to do the same.

29

Old clothes

We often throw away old clothes because they are out of fashion. But they may not be worn out and could be used again. Try and take your old clothes to a charity shop or give them to a jumble sale.

Some old clothes can be pulled apart and made into new clothes. The woollen fibres from woollen clothes can be re-spun and made into new yarn. Cotton clothes can be used to make high-quality paper. And artificial materials such as nylon can be used to make the stuffing for furniture and roofing felt.

Recycling clothes saves raw materials and saves space on landfill sites.

The old clothes sold at charity ▶ shops can raise money for the work of the charity. Or they can be sent to countries where people need the clothes.

New things from old

So many of the things we throw away could be used again. Before you throw something away, think about what will happen to it. See if you can re-use it, recycle it or make it into something else. Remember that wastes do not just disappear when you throw them away. Most of the different methods of getting rid of wastes harm the environment. Making things from new materials also uses up valuable energy and raw materials.

◀ Can you design and make something entirely from waste materials?

The sandals on sale in ▶ this market in Bolivia, South America, have been made from old car tyres. Car tyres are hard to get rid of. If they are not burnt in a special, high temperature incinerator, harmful gases are released into the air.

Useful Addresses

If you would like to find out more about the ideas in this book, write to any of these organisations:

Aluminium Can Recycling Association, I-MEX House, 52 Blucher Street, Birmingham B1 1QU.

British Glass, Northumberland Road, Sheffield, S10 2UA.

British Plastics Federation, 5 Belgrave Square, London SW1X 8PD.

British Steel Tinplate, P. O. Box No. 101 Velindre, Swansea, West Glamorgan, SA5 5WW.

British Waste Paper Association, Alexander House Business Centre, Station Road, Aldershot, Hants, GU11 1BQ.

Council for Environmental Education, School of Education, University of Reading, London Road, Reading, RG1 5AQ.

Friends of the Earth (UK), 26–28 Underwood Street, London N1 7JQ.

Friends of the Earth (Australia), Chain Reaction Co-operative, P. O. Box 530E, Melbourne, Victoria 3001.

Friends of the Earth (New Zealand), P. O. Box 39–065, Auckland West.

Greenpeace (UK), 30–31 Islington Green, London N1 8XE.

Greenpeace (Australia), Studio 14, 37 Nicholson Street, Balmain, New South Wales 2041.

Greenpeace (New Zealand), Private Bag, Wellesley Street, Auckland.

The Tidy Britain Group, The Pier, Wigan, WN3 4EX.

UK Atomic Energy Authority Education Service, International Teaching Resource Centre, P. O. Box 5, Wetherby, Yorkshire, LS23 7EH.

UK Reclamation Council, 16 High Street, Brampton, Huntingdon, Cambridgeshire, PE18 8TU.

Waste Watch, NCVO, 26 Bedford Square, London, WC1B 3HU.

Watch, 22 The Green, Nettleham, Lincoln, LN2 2NR.

World-Wide Fund for Nature (WWF), Panda House, Weyside Park, Godalming, Surrey, GU7 1XR.

Index

aluminium 24, 25
animal waste 16, 17, 19

bacteria 7, 8, 17
bags 5
batteries 12
beaches 15, 17
biodegradable materials 7–9
bio-gas chambers 16
birds 12, 15
bottle banks 27, 28

cans 24, 25
cars 21, 26
car tyres 31
chemical waste 14, 24
compost heap 9, 12
crops 4, 16, 17, 19
cullet 27

decomposers 7, 8, 9, 16, 19
disease 10, 12, 13, 16, 17
dog dirt 16
dung 16, 19

electricity from rubbish 13
electric vehicles 11

energy 18, 20, 21, 24, 25, 26, 28, 31

factories 4, 20, 21, 25–28
farm animals 4, 16
feathers 15
food 5, 6, 7, 9
fuel 20
fungi 7, 8

glass 6, 7, 27, 28

household rubbish 6

incinerators 13, 14, 19, 29, 31

landfill site 12, 19, 21, 30
leaf litter 8
litter 4, 10, 11

magnets 24, 26
metals 6, 7, 18, 24, 25, 26
methane gas 12, 16
mines 4, 24

nuclear waste 14

oil 14, 15, 28, 29

packaging 5, 6, 29
paper 6, 7, 18, 20–23, 30
plant waste 8, 9
plastics 6, 7, 10, 29
poisonous waste 4, 12, 14, 15, 19, 20
pollution 10, 12, 13, 14, 15, 18, 20, 21, 24, 29, 31

radioactive waste 14
raw materials 18, 20, 24, 25, 26, 28, 29, 30, 31
recycling 4, 13, 17, 18, 19, 21–31
rivers 17, 20, 21, 24

scrap metal 26
sea 15, 17, 19
sewage 4, 17, 19
shopping 5
soil 7, 8, 9, 10, 12, 14, 16, 24
steel 24, 26
street cleaning 11

transport 20, 21, 25, 27, 28
trees 8, 18, 20, 21

water 17
wildlife 10, 15